STRATEGIC ANALYSIS

B. Hiriyappa

Contents of The Book

1	Strategic Analysis	1 To 7
2	Situational Analysis	8 To 12
3	The Methods Of Industry And Competitive Analysis	13 To 18
4	Strategic Groups	19 To 26
5	SWOT Analysis	27 To 38
6	Tows Matrix Analysis	39 To 45
7	BCG Matrix	46 To 57

B Hiriyappa

Dedicated To Readers Who Read This Book

CHAPTER 1
STRATEGIC ANALYSIS

"Analysis is the critical starting point of strategic thinking"
Kenichi Ohmae

"If you're not faster than your competitor, you're in a tenuous position, and if you're only half as fast, you're terminal"
George Salk

"The idea is to concentrate our strength against our competitor's relative weakness"
Bruce Henderson

INTRODUCTION

In this chapter, we shall discuss about the strategic analysis and its tools, major issues consider for strategic analysis, situational analysis, the methods of industry and competitive analysis, the concept of strategic groups, SWOT analysis and portfolio analysis. The strategic management process includes a set of managerial decisions and actions which determined the long term planning and effective performance of superior objectives and goals of the organization. It involves important aspects like setting the organization's mission, vision, company or organization profile, external environment, operating industry, multinational analysis, developing objectives, development of strategic analysis and choice and implementing the strategies, to the accomplishment of the long term objectives and short-term objectives and finally control, monitor, guidance and evaluation of organization objectives.

STRATEGIC ANALYSIS

SWOT is the heart of Strategic Analysis. SWOT analysis is the process of carefully inspecting the business and its environment through the various dimensions like Strengths, Weaknesses, Opportunities and Threats. Strengths are referred to the company's core competencies, and it includes proprietary technology, skills, resources, market position, patents, and others. These are analyzing the strength of businesses' position and understanding the important external factors that may influence that to company's position.

Strategy formulation is not a task in which strategic managers can be gotten by opinions, good instincts, and creative thinking from the strategic managers in the company. Strategic analysis solidly based on the company's internal and external environment situation. It includes:

❖ Industry and competitive conditions
❖ A company's core competitive capabilities, resources, internal strengths and weakness and market situations about the company.

These are the most important situational considerations in strategic analysis. The process of company's strategic analysis will be assisted by the PEST Analysis, Scenario Analysis, Five Forces Analysis, Market Segmentation, And Directional Policy Matrix, Competitor Analysis, Critical Successes Factor Analysis, SWOT Analysis, Strategic Choice, And Strategy Implementation.

STRATEGIC ANALYSIS TOOLS

Strategic Analysis Tools Are PEST Analysis, Scenario Analysis, Five Forces Analysis, Market Segmentation, And Directional Policy Matrix, Competitor Analysis, Critical Successes Factor Analysis, SWOT Analysis, Strategic Choice, And Strategy Implementation. These strategic analysis tools are discussed below:

PEST Analysis

It is a technique for understanding the "environment" factors like politics, Economic, Social and Technology in which a business operates.

Scenario Planning

It is a technique that builds various plausible views of possible futures for a business.

Five Forces Analysis

It is a technique for identifying the forces which affect the level of competition in an industry level and business level.

Market Segmentation

It is a technique which seeks to identify similarities and differences between groups of customers or users of company's products and services.

Directional Policy Matrix

It is a technique which summarizes the competitive strength of a business's operation in specific markets and specific nature of business in different markets.

Competitor Analysis

It is a wide range of techniques and analysis that seeks to summarize a businesses' overall competitive position in business level and industry level.

Critical Success Factor Analysis

It is a technique to identify those areas in which a business must outperform the competition in order to succeed in the market and business.

SWOT Analysis

It is a useful summary technique for summarizing the key issues arising from an assessment of a business's "internal" position and "external" environmental influences to the company.

Strategic Choice

This process involves understanding the nature of stakeholder expectations along with identifying strategic options, and then evaluating and selecting strategic options in the business.

Strategy Implementation

It is often the hardest part in strategic analysis. When a strategy has been analyzed and selected, this task is ready to translate it into organizational action.

ISSUES TO CONSIDER FOR STRATEGIC ANALYSES

Strategy evolves over a period of time and it considers major issues that will be relevant to strategic analysis as outlined:

- ❖ Different forces which are driven and constrain in the company and that must be balanced in strategic decisions will be made by strategic managers.
- ❖ It is to be considering the possible implications of routine decisions in a company environment.
- ❖ It is the results of a series of small decisions are taken over an extended period of time in an organization.

❖ An organization manager effort to increase the growth momentum   which happens apart from the changing strategy.

Balance

❖ The process of strategy formulation is often explained as one of the matching the internal core potential of the company with the utilization of opportunities.

❖ Strategic analysis is to involve a workable balance between diversity and conflicting considerations in organizing.

❖ A strategic manager in an organization has responsibilities to make decisions that are balancing the opportunities, influences, threats and constraints.

❖ Pressures in the organization are driving towards a particular choice like entering a new market.

❖ The major constraints existed in organizations like existence of big competition in the market.

❖ Strategic constraints will be produced and   an impact on the organization in terms of changes in nature, degree, magnitude and its importance in an organization.

❖ These mentioned issues are some extent to manage by strategic managers in the company. Apart from the several issues are beyond the control of a manager in an organization.

Risk

❖ Maintaining balance is very important to an organization.

❖ The complexities and intermingling of variables in the environment which reduces the strategic balances in the organization. It will be a major risk to strategic managers.

❖ Risk is uncertain and the business is of no exception.

❖ Risks are competitive markets, liberalization, globalizations, booms, recessions, technological advancement and intercompany relationships are affecting business and pose a risk at varying degree which depends on the nature of problems.

❖ Strategic analysis is to identify potential imbalances or risks and assess their consequences.

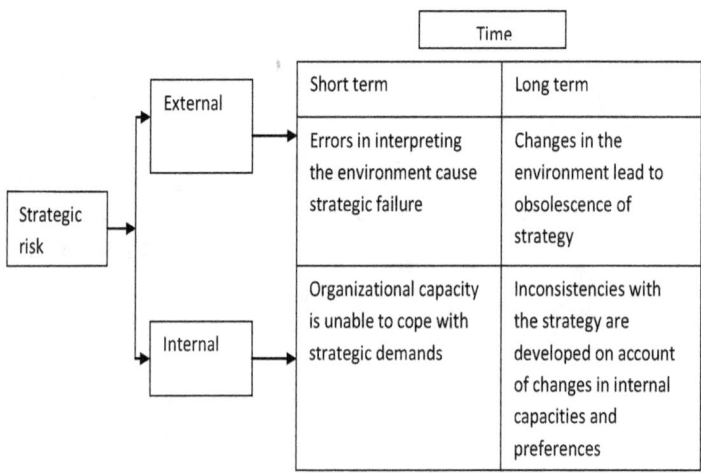

	Time	
	Short term	Long term
External	Errors in interpreting the environment cause strategic failure	Changes in the environment lead to obsolescence of strategy
Internal	Organizational capacity is unable to cope with strategic demands	Inconsistencies with the strategy are developed on account of changes in internal capacities and preferences

Strategic risk

❖ External risks are inconsistencies between strategies and forces in the environment.

❖ Internal risks occur on account of forces either within the environment or are directly interacting with the organization on the programme basis (routine basis).

CHAPTER 2
SITUATIONAL ANALYSIS

INTRODUCTION

- ❖ Situational analysis is to influence internal and external environment of the organization or company or business enterprises.
- ❖ Internal environment analysis of the strength and weakness of the firm.
- ❖ External environment analysis of the opportunities and threats of the firm.
- ❖ Macro environmental factors like demographic, economic, social values and lifestyles, governmental and regulation, technological factors.
- ❖ The company's macro environment includes the all the relevant factors and influences to firm within outside boundaries of the organization.
- ❖ Situational analysis is the analysis of the internal and external environment factors for making the decisions of the company towards its direction, objectives, strategy and its business model.
- ❖ It watchful eye to see what is happening in the outside forces of the firm and make a proper assessment of the opportunities and threats of the organization.
- ❖ Strategic managers are ready to scan the external environment of the company and they must watch potential important environment forces and assess their impact and its influence of business, and will be adapted in from the form proper direction: this purpose strategy is needed in business.
- ❖ Development of appropriate and suitable business strategy which is based from the forces such as macro environment that will be shaped and impact immediately industry and competitive environment.

These are almost certainly pertaining to the impact of the enterprise.

Figure – 2.1: From Thinking Strategically about the Company's Situation to Choosing a Strategy

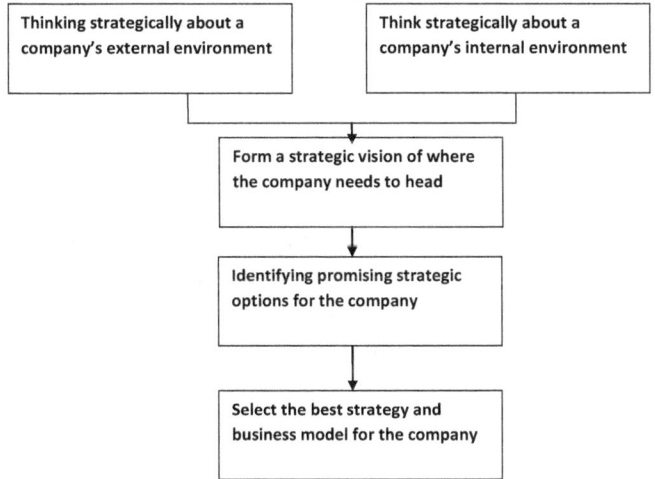

Figure 2.1 clearly outlined from thinking strategically about the company's situation to choosing a strategy:

❖ Before development of marketing strategy, it is very important to conduct some form analyses which are helpful for the development of marketing strategy in the company.

❖ It should be an essential part of a business plan and should be reviewed over time in this way ensure its current situation in business.

❖ Many tasks are helpful to conduct an analysis of the raw introduction of strategy and provide a checklist of the most important factors to take into account for the development of marketing strategies in enterprise as listed below:

Product Situation

- ❖ Strategic consultant should know the current products and services which are offered by the company.
- ❖ The strategic manager should know the core products and subsidiary/supporting/secondary products and services available in the market.
- ❖ Strategist observes that company's products and services that are meeting the core clients' needs in market.

Competitive Situation

- ❖ Who are main competitors and what are the main competitive products and services in the market?
- ❖ What are competitive advantages of competitors?
- ❖ What is the competition level in the industry?

Distribution Situation

- ❖ What are channels available for distribution of products and services?
- ❖ How are you getting your product to market?
- ❖ Do you need to go through different distributors or other intermediaries?

Opportunity and Issue Analysis

- ❖ What are the current opportunities for the company?
- ❖ What are future opportunities for the company?
- ❖ What are the current threats to the company?
- ❖ What are the future challenges for the company?
- ❖ How to faces challenges in company?
- ❖ Framework of strategic analysis is the starting point of strategic management.

- ❖ Industries widely differ in terms of economic characteristics, competitive situations, and future profit prospects.

- ❖ Economic characters vary in industries according to factors like overall size and market growth rate.

- ❖ Pace of the technological change in industries.

- ❖ The geographical boundaries of market extended to worldwide.

- ❖ Increases the buyer and sellers of the similar products and differentiated,

- ❖ Economies scales help to industries to face cut throat competition in the industry.

- ❖ Different types of distribution channels which accessed and used by buyers and industries.

- ❖ Industries competition focuses on the best competitive prices for the products and services which are available very competitive price to customers.

- ❖ Industries offers new product features and new performance to customers.

- ❖ Strategy frameworks help to create brand reputation in the market.

- ❖ It creates challenges and smoothly and cooperation with the company and its suppliers and customers.

- ❖ Competitive situation innovation of new products and services in different market in the world.

Figure – 2.2: Framework of Strategic Analysis

```
                    ┌─────────────────────┐
                    │  Strategic Analysis │
                    └─────────────────────┘
                              │
              ┌───────────────┴───────────────┐
              ▼                                ▼
   ┌──────────────────┐           ┌──────────────────┐
   │ External Analysis│           │ Internal Analysis│
   └──────────────────┘           └──────────────────┘
              │                                │
              ▼                                ▼
```

External Analysis	Internal Analysis
❖ **Customer Analysis** Segments, motivations, unmet needs	❖ Performance Allowance Profitability, sales, shareholders value analysis, customer satisfaction, product quality, brand associations, relative cost, new products, employee capability and performance and product portfolio analysis.
❖ **Competitor Analysis** Identity, strategic groups, performance, image, objectives, strategies , culture, cost structure, strengths, weaknesses.	❖ Determinates Analysis Past and current strategies, strategic problems, organizational capabilities and constraints, financial resources and constraints, strengths, and weaknesses.
❖ **Market Analysis** Size, projected growth, profitability, entry, barriers, cost structure, strengths, weaknesses	
❖ **Environment Analysis** Technological , government, economic, demographic, scenarios, information needed areas	

Strategic strengths, weakness, problems, constraints, and uncertainties

Opportunities, threats, trends and strategic, uncertainties

Strategy Identification and Selection

 ❖ Identify strategic alternatives
  ▪ Product maker investment strategies
  ▪ Functional areas strategies
  ▪ Assets, competencies and synergies
 ❖ Select strategy
 ❖ Implement the operating plan
 ❖ Review Strategies

CHAPTER 3
THE METHODS OF
INDUSTRY AND
COMPETITIVE ANALYSIS

INTRODUCTION

Industry analysis begins with a definition of products and markets, skills and competitors contained within the industry, followed by industry structural analysis, and concluded with the identification of the key success factors for the industry. The methods of industry and competitive analysis are listed below:

- ❖ Industry and competitive analysis will be done using a set of concepts, and techniques.

- ❖ Industry can be set a fix and a clear key trait industry for identifying different drivers of the industry.

- ❖ Competitive analysis determines market positions and strategies of rival companies.

- ❖ The key success of the industry is its profit outlook.

- ❖ The industry and its competitive analysis provide a route for thinking strategically about industries overall situation and drawing conclusions relating about whether industry represents an attractive investment for company funds.

- ❖ It examines a company's business in the context of internal and external environment.

❖ Industry and competitive analysis aims at developing insight on several issues fix it, to know the intensity of competition, to analyze the degree of change drivers.

Analyzing these issues have built and an understanding of an enterprise environment and of industry and competitive analysis issues is outlined:

Dominant Economic Features of the Industry

The industry is significantly different from their basic character and structure. Industry and competitive analysis have an overview of the industry's and its firm's dominant economic features. The industry is "a group of firms whose products have same and similar attributes such that they compete for the same buyers". Dominant economic features of the industry as listed below:

❖ Market size.

❖ Scope of competitive rivalry with local, regional, national, international, or global.

❖ Market growth rate and its position like early development, rapid growth, and take off, early maturity, saturation, and stagnation, decline in business life.

❖ Number of rivals and their relative sizes in market.

❖ What are the smallest and dominant companies?

❖ Number of buyers and their relative sizes and know the extent industry rivals have integrated in terms of backward or forward or both.

❖ To know the types of distribution channels used to access customers in the market.

❖ To know the pace of technological changes in terms of production process innovation and new product introductions.

❖ To know the products and services of rival firms are highly differentiated, weakly differentiated or essentially identical.

❖ To know the companies economies of scale in terms of purchasing, manufacturing, transportation, marketing and advertising.

❖ To know the key industry participants are clustered in a particular location. For instance, lock industry in Aligarh, Sarees and diamonds in Surat, Information Technology in Bangalore, Hyderabad, and Noida; similarly, there is also a concentration of business in different countries on account of geographical and other reasons.

❖ To know the high rates of capacity utilization are crucial to achieving low cost production efficiency.

❖ Capital requirement of the company and easy of entry and exit in market.

❖ To know the industry profitability is above or below par value of the share.

Nature and Strength of Competition

❖ Industry and competitive analysis investigation into industry's competitive process. It discovers the main sources of competitive pressure and analyzes the how they are strong in each competitive force in the industry.

❖ This step is essential and basic requirement of the mangers for formulation of successful strategy, Strategic manager cannot create a successful strategy without in depth understanding of the industry's competitive character.

❖ Competitive pressures in various industries are not same.

❖ Competitive process works in similarly enough to use a common analytical framework in gauging the nature and intensity of competitive forces.

❖ Competitive analysis is the powerful tool for systematically diagnosing the principle competitive pressures in a market and assessing competitive strengths how is strong and how is important.

❖ Competitive analysis is easy to understand and apply to the firm's environment.

Triggers of Change

Industry economic features and competitive structure explain about its fundamental character relating to changing ways of environmental factors. The industry is ready to adjust changes in its activities. Changes will be occurred in internally or externally. Industrialized economy and competitive forces are ready to face constraints from changes which either relevant to business or not relevant force of the business. Industries character and trends and new development in the market will be gradually produce changes. These are important and enough to require a strategic response from participating firms in the market. Popular hypothesis enable to industries and its life cycle going through changes and it explains the reasons for changing of the life cycle. Industry life cycle strongly key changes of the growth rate of industry and business enterprise. When changing the industry and business activities that time ready to face serious and constraint problems with enterprise.

The Concept of Driving Force

- ❖ The concept of driving force is the most important to judge what growth stage an industry is.

- ❖ It is identifying the more analytical value relating to the specific factors that are causing fundamental industry and competitive adjustment analysis.

- ❖ Industry and competitive conditions are changed due to pressure, motion by creating incentives.

- ❖ The most dominant and important forces in the enterprise are called as driving force.

- ❖ It is the biggest influence of different kinds of changes will be taking place in the industry's structure and competitive environment.

Analyzing driving forces have involved two steps:

1. Identifying what are the driving forces in the industry.

2. Assessment and what are the impact of the driving forces in the industry.

The Most Common Driving Force

Many and powerful events will be affected an industry, apart from industry powerfully enough to quality as driving forces. Some of driving forces are unique and specific to a particular industry situation. Therefore, many driving forces are changing nature, these are falling into the general category that affecting different industries simultaneously. Important and most common driving forces are outlined:

- ❖ The internet and new e-commerce opportunities and threats it breeds in the industry.

- ❖ Increasing globalization and liberalization.

- ❖ Changes in the long term industry growth rate of firms.

- ❖ Product innovation in firms.

- ❖ Market innovation in industry.

- ❖ Entry or exit of major firms in markets.

- ❖ Technology transfer.

- ❖ Effective changes in terms of cost and efficiency.

Identifying the Companies That Are In the Strongest / Weakest Position

The next step is to be examining the industry's competitive structure of the firm; it is to study the market positions of rival firms in the market. The strategic grouping technique is one of the important and dominant techniques that revealing the competitive positions of firms. Strategic grouping techniques are one of the useful analytical tools for comparing the market positions of each Firm separately or forming a group of firms. It is very difficult to assess and examine to each firm competitor and competitive positions in the market.

CHAPTER 4

STRATEGIC GROUPS

THE CONCEPT OF STRATEGIC GROUPS

Generally, an industry often differs from each other with respect to several factors like distribution channels used, market segment served, product quality, technological leadership, customer service, pricing policy, advertising policy and promotions, within most industries. It is possible to observe groups of organization in which each member follows the same basic strategy as other organizations in the group but strategy is different from the one followed by companies in other groups. A strategic group principally consists of those rival firms with similar competitive approaches and positions in the market. These groups of organizations are known as strategic groups.

Normally, a limited number of groups capture the essence of the strategic difference between companies with an industry.

Implications of Strategic Groups

The concept of strategic groups has a number of

19

implications for industry analysis and the identification of opportunities and threats are as outlined.

❖ Organization immediate competitors are those in its strategic groups. Since all the organizations in a strategic groups are pursuing similar strategies, consumer tend to view the products of such organization as being a direct substitute for each other thus major threat to a company is profitability can come from within its own strategic groups.

❖ Different strategic groups can have a different standing with respect to each of Porter's five competitive forces. It means, that, the risk of new entry by potential competitors, the degree of rivalry among organizations within a group, the bargaining power of suppliers, and the competitive force of substitute products can all vary in intensity among different strategic groups within the same industry.

❖ Identify the competitive characteristics that differentiate firms in the industry. It is typical variables like price, quality range in the form of high, medium, and low; geographic coverage in the form of local, regional, national and global; degree of vertical integration like none, partial, full; product line breadth in terms of wide and narrow; use of distribution channels in the form of one, any and all; and degree of services offered like no – frills, limited, and full.

❖ Assigns similar services and products firms that fall in about the same strategy space for the same strategic group.

❖ Plot the firms on a two variable map and its using pairs in different characteristics.

❖ Draw circles around each strategic group in this way make the circles that proportional to the size of the groups. These groups have respective share of total industry sales revenues.

❖ The above mentioned procedures for constructing a strategic group map and deciding that firms belong in which strategic group have straightforward.

Likely Strategic Moves of Rivals

❖ The firm always watching what is doing their competitors in the market. Unless if the firm is neglected their competitors. Its impact on firm businesses, profit, and growth rate and end up its competitive battle in a market.

❖ A company cannot expect to competitor result without proper monitoring their actions, understanding their strategies and future anticipating moves.

❖ Company watches their competitor just like as a spy.

❖ Company watch competitors' latest strategies, moves, forces, growth, development, alliances, joint venture, technology innovations, strategic alliances with partners, core competencies, core resources, core strengths and weakness of their competitors.

Key factors for competitive success

Industries Key Success Factors are those factors that most affect the industry and its members able to prosper their market place:

❖ Particularly relating with strategy elements, product attributes core resources, competencies, competitive capabilities, and business outcomes that associated between profit and loss.

❖ Competitive success factors are very important in all kinds of business enterprises.

❖ Competitive success factors will be shaping the company will be financially strong and competitively successful in local, national and international market.

Industries Key Success Factors

The primary purpose of industry analysis is to identify the requirements and trends that determine the key success factors for the business. The key determinant success factor in the industry   as listed below:

❖ Customer requirements,

❖ Competitive factors that must be met,

❖ Regulations/industry standards in the business,

❖ The resource requirements implement competitive strategy, and others.

❖ Technical requirements to build a competitive position.

❖ It may be used to identify the internal strengths and weaknesses of the organization.

❖ It can be scrutinized industry competitors, as well as customer needs, vertical industry structures, channels of distribution costs barriers to entry, availability of substitutes, and supplier.

❖ A strategist seeks to determine whether organization's current internal capabilities represent strengths or weakness in the new competitive factors.

Apparel Industries Key Success Factors

Apparel industries key success factors are appealing designs and color combinations which create only on buyer interest and low cost manufacturing efficiency to permit attractive retail pricing and ample to improve margins of profit.

Tin and Aluminum Cans

Tin and aluminum cans key success factors are the cost of shipping empty cans is substantial, and another factor is the plant located close to end use customers so that the plant's output can be marketed within economical shipping distances to regional market share is far more crucial than national share.

Determining the Industry's Key Success Factors

- ❖ To know the prevailing and the anticipation competitive condition.

- ❖ To give top priority for analytical consideration.

- ❖ Strategic managers understand the industry situation and less than competitive successes.

- ❖ Strategic managers pay attention to the kinds of resources and its competitive valuable.

- ❖ Give training to strategic managers for improvement of competitive skills.

- ❖ Acquired stronger market position

- ❖ Efforts better than rivals for gaining competitive advantage that is one of the golden opportunities of the firms.

❖ Industry's key success factors are the cornerstone of the company's strategy and trying to gain sustainable competitive advantage.

Prospectus and Financial Attractiveness of Industry

The final step of industry and competitive analysis is to use the outcome of the analysis have drawn conclusions about the relative attractiveness or unattractiveness of the industry. The analysis is to be either short or long term that depends on industry circumstances. Strategist has responsible person to assess the industry outlook carefully, deciding about present industry and competitive conditions in a company in this way attractive business opportunity for the growth, development, survival, earning of profits that can be gloomy prospect. Important prospectus and financial attractiveness of industry as listed below:

❖ The industry's growth potential rate.

❖ The industry's profitable is favorable or unfavorable that affected by the prevailing driving force of the company.

❖ Currently rivalry permits to companies earn adequate profitability and competitive forces will become very stronger compare to walk.

❖ The company's competitive position in the industry and its position are likely to grow in terms of stronger or weaker.

❖ The companies potential to convert into weak competitive position into a strong competitive position in this way achieve the mission and vision of the company.

- ❖ Companies able to build up counteract policy to unattractive situation convert into an attractive situation in the company.

- ❖ Reduce the degree of risk and make certainty in future company business.

- ❖ The severity of constraints which confronting the industry as a whole.

- ❖ The company continued participation in business activities and it is very important and able to cope and use resources successfully for the business interest.

- ❖ A general concept relating to the industry: If an industry's overall profit prospects are above average, the industry can be considered attractive: if its profit prospectus is below average, which time it is unattractive. Therefore, strategist makes the mistake to evaluate the industries as being attractive or unattractive to all type industry participants and all potential entrants. The term attractiveness is relative and not absolute. Industry environment is unattractive to weak competitors may be attractive to strong competitors in the market.

Assessment of industry enhances to fundamental attractiveness relating to current industry participants who are employed strategies for calculated to strengthen in a long term competitive position of business, expansion of business in terms of sales, investment, additional facilities and modern equipment which are needed in the industry.

In the case, the industry and competitive situation are judged as unattractive, this time more successful industry participants may be chosen cautiously to invest, look for different ways to protect their long term competitiveness and profitability of the business. If the company is strong that time company is ready to acquire smaller firms and diversified their business activities and convert into a successful business venture. In the case weak companies, these are considered to be unattractive industry. These are merging with a rival to strengthen the market share and profitability or alternatively looking for outside industry for attractive diversification and its new opportunities properly utilized by weak industries.

CHAPTER 5
SWOT ANALYSIS

INTRODUCTION

SWOT is the heart of Strategic Analysis. SWOT analysis is the process of carefully inspecting the business and its environment through the various dimensions of Strengths, Weaknesses, Opportunities, and Threats. SWOT" is an acronym which represents "Strengths", "Weaknesses", "Opportunities", and "Threats".

Strengths

Strengths are the companies' core competencies, and include proprietary technology, skills, resources, market position, patents, and others. Strengths are an inherent capability of the organization. And it can be used to gain strategic advantage over its competitors in the business.

Weaknesses

Weaknesses are conditions within the company that can lead to poor performance, and can include obsolete equipment, heavy debt burden, poor product or market image, weak management, and others. A weakness is an inherent limitation or problems of the organization. And it creates strategic disadvantages to business enterprise.

Opportunities

Opportunities are outside conditions or circumstances that the company could turn to its advantage, and could include a specialty niche skill or technology that suddenly realizes a growth in broad market interest. An opportunity is a favorable condition of the organization's environment. And it enables to be strengthening its position in the business.

Threats

Threats are current or future conditions in the outside environment that may harm the company, and might include population shifts, purchasing preferences, new technologies, or an increase in competition. A treat is unfavorable condition in the organization's environment that causes a risk for, or damage to the organization's position in the market.

SWOT analysis is to identify the strategies that will create a firm specific business model that will best support, it fit, or match a firm's resources and capabilities to the demands of the environment in which enterprise operates. Strategic managers compare and find the gap the various alternative possible strategies against each other with respect to enterprise ability to accomplish major goals and superior profitability of the firm's. The strategic manager identifies the set of strategies that will be created and sustain a competitive advantage in the form of functional level, business level, global, corporate level, and operational strategy.

Functional Level Strategy

It's directed towards to the effectiveness of operations within the company in terms of manufacturing, marketing, material management, product development and customer services.

Corporate level Strategy

It is concerned with the overall purpose and scope of the business to meet its stakeholder expectations. This is a crucial level since it is heavily influenced by investors in the business and acts to guide strategic decision-making throughout the business. Corporate strategy is often stated explicitly in a "mission statement" of the company. It focuses on the maximization of the long term profitability of the company. It enhances to increase the market share and business development process in the market.

Business level Strategy

It is concerned more with how a business competes successfully in a particular market. It concerns strategic decisions about choice of products, meeting the needs of customers, gaining advantage over competitors, exploiting or creating new opportunities etc.

Operational Strategy

It is concerned with how each part of the business is organized to deliver the corporate and business-unit level strategic direction. Operational strategy therefore focuses on issues of resources, processes, and people etc.

Global Strategy

It is addressing how to expand business operations outside the home country to grow and prosper in a world where competitive advantage is determined at a global level.

The organization performs in the marketplace is significantly influenced by the three dominant factors are listed below:

- ❖ The organization's correct market position
- ❖ The nature of environmental opportunities and threats
- ❖ The organizations resource capability to capitalize the opportunities and its ability to protect against the threat.

Significance of SWOT Analysis

The Major significance of a SWOT analysis   as outlined:

It provides a logical Framework

- ❖ It provides a logical framework for systematic and sound approachable issues having a bearing on the business situation.

- ❖ It helps in the generation of alternative strategies and the choice of a strategy.

- ❖ Different managerial perceptions relating about organizational strengths and weaknesses and the environmental opportunities an threat that leads to differences is approaching to specific strategies and finally determine the choice of strategy. It takes place through an interactive process in dynamic backdrop in business.

It Presents a Comparative Account

- ❖ It presents the information about both external and internal environments in a structured form.

- ❖ It's possible to compare external opportunities and threats along with internal strengths and weaknesses.

- ❖ It helps strategist to form a suitable strategy that matching to internal and external environment factors of companies.

- ❖ The pattern of strengths, weakness, opportunity and threats are comparing with from one to another.

It Guides the Strategist in Strategy Identification

- ❖ Strategist can be faced problems when the organization cannot match in the SWOT pattern.

- ❖ An organization must have certain opportunities along with the specific threats; it is equally true that, the organization may have powerful strengths coupled with major weaknesses in the light of the critical success factors.

❖ SWOT analysis is guided to strategist to think about the organization overall position that helps strategist to identify the major purpose of the strategy under focus in business.

❖ SWOT analysis helps to strategic managers to craft a business model. It will allow to company to gain competitive advantages from its industries. Competitive advantage leads to be increased profitability, and maximizes a company's chances of survival in the fast changing, global competitive environment that characteristics of most industries today. Changing of environment, a company constantly develops a marketing information system to track relevant trends and developments. These can be categorized as an opportunity and a threat.

Figure -5.1: SWOT Analysis: What to Look for in Sizing Up A Company's Strengths, Weakness, Opportunities, and Threats

Potential Resources Strengths and competitive capabilities	Potential Resources Weaknesses and Competitive Deficiencies
A	B
Potential Company Opportunities	Potential External Threats to Company's Well – Being
C	D

Part – A: Potential Resources Strengths and competitive capabilities

❖ A powerful strategy which is supported by competitively valuable skills and experience in the key areas infirm.

- ❖ A stronger financial condition which helpful to grow the business.

- ❖ Brand reputation and company image.

- ❖ A widely recognized market leader in the market and an attractive customer base to firm.

- ❖ Ability to take advantage of economies scale in the production of goods and services.

- ❖ Advanced and superior skills in technology.

- ❖ Cost advantages of firm.

- ❖ Strong and advertising network of firm.

- ❖ New product innovation skills of firm.

- ❖ Ability to has proven skills in improving product quality process.

- ❖ Sophisticated use of e–technologies and relating communication processes.

- ❖ Superior skills in supply chain management of firm.

- ❖ A reputation of good customer services of firm.

- ❖ Better product quality relative to their competitor.

- ❖ Wide geographic coverage and strong global distribution capability of firm.

- ❖ Strategic alliances, joint ventures with other firms that provide to access valuable technology, competencies, core distribution channels, products and services and attractive geographic markets.

Part – B: Potential Resources Weaknesses and Competitive Deficiencies

- ❖ No clear strategic decisions in business.

- ❖ Obsolete facilities of firm

- ❖ Weak financial position and heavy burdened too much debt of firm.

- ❖ Firm's unit cost higher than competitor price.

- ❖ Missing the core competences.

- ❖ Deficiencies in terms of skills, intellectual property capital relative leading rivals in market.

- ❖ No cost control measure of firm.

- ❖ Plagued with internal operational problems of the firm.

- ❖ Falling behind rivals in putting e- commerce capability and strengths of a   firm.

- ❖ To narrow a product line relative to rivals of the firm.

- ❖ Short on financial resources to fund which promising strategic initiative of the firm.

- ❖ Not attracting new customers   as rapidly as rivals in the market,

- ❖ Leaving of experienced, trained and skilled employees from the firm.

- ❖ Inadequate distribution channels of firm.

Part - C: Potential Company Opportunities

- ❖ Expansion of business activities in this way getting of additional customer base to firm.

- ❖ Expansion of product segments

- ❖ Expanding the firm's product line and meet the requirement the broader range of customer needs in market.

- ❖ Effective utilization of existing skills and technologies for how to enter new markets with new product and services.

- ❖ Using the internet and e- commerce network communications and technologies to dramatically cut costs in this way pursue new sales growth opportunities.

- ❖ Integration of backward and forward diversification of business.

- ❖ Falling trade barriers in attractive foreign markets of firms.

- ❖ The firm's ability to market share from rival firms in the market.

- ❖ Firm able to grow rapidly in the form of rising demand from customers in different countries.

- ❖ Acquisitions of rival industries in market with technological expertise of firms.

- ❖ Strategic alliances and joint venture of firms that expand the firm's market share, customer base and its competitive capabilities and core competencies.

- ❖ Firms are opening to exploit emerging market due to new technologies.

- ❖ Firms enhance their brand image and company reputation.

Part – D : Potential External Threats to Company's Well – Being

- ❖ Likely entry of potential new customers in market.

- ❖ Loss of sales to substitute products in markets

- ❖ Mounting competition from new internet startup companies pursuing e – commerce strategies in their business.

❖ Increasing the intensity of the firm's competition in the market.

❖ Technological change's impact of product demand reduced from customers.

❖ Slowdown in market growth of firms.

❖ The adverse impact of foreign exchange rates and trade policies of foreign governments which affected to firm's business operation.

❖ New Government regulatory requirements.

❖ Growing bargaining powers of customers and vendors in the market.

❖ Adverse demographic changes which threaten to curtail demand for the firm's products and services.

❖ Major vulnerability to industry driving forces.

SWOT ANALYSIS OF INDIAN DAIRY INDUSTRY

Strengths:	Weaknesses:
• **Demand profile:** Absolutely optimistic. • **Margins:** Quite reasonable, even on packed liquid milk. • **Flexibility of product mix:** Tremendous. With balancing equipment, you can keep on adding to your product line. • **Availability of raw material:** Abundant. Presently, more than 80 per cent of milk produced is flowing into the unorganized sector, which requires proper channelization.	• **Perish ability:** Pasteurization has overcome this weakness partially. UHT gives milk long life. Surely, many new processes will follow to improve milk quality and extend its shelf life. • **Lack of control over yield:** Theoretically, there is little control over milk yield. However, increased awareness of developments like embryo transplant, artificial insemination and properly managed animal husbandry practices, coupled with higher income to rural milk producers

Technical manpower: Professionally-trained, technical human resource pool, built over last 30 years.	should automatically lead to improvement in milk yields. • **The logistics of procurement:** Woes of bad roads and inadequate transportation facility make milk procurement problematic. But with the overall economic improvement in India, these problems would also get solved. • **Problematic distribution:** Yes, all is not well with the distribution. But then if ice creams can be sold virtually at every nook and corner, why can't we sell other dairy products too? Moreover, it is only a matter of time before we see the emergence of a cold chain linking the producer to the refrigerator at the consumer's home! **Competition:** With so many newcomers entering this industry, competition becomes tougher day by day. But then competition has to be faced as a ground reality. The market is large enough for many to carve out their niche.
Opportunities:	Threats:
"Failure is never final, and success never ending". Dr Kurien bears out this	Milk vendors, the un-organized sector: Today milk vendors are occupying the pride of place in

statement perfectly. He entered the industry when there were only threats. He met failure head-on, and now he clearly is an example of 'never ending success'! If dairy entrepreneurs are looking for opportunities in India, the following areas must be tapped:

Value addition: There is a phenomenal scope for innovations in product development, packaging and presentation. Given below are potential areas of value addition:

Steps should be taken to introduce value-added products like Shrikhand, ice creams, pioneer, Chou, flavored milk, dairy sweets, etc. This will lead to a greater presence and flexibility in the market place along with opportunities in the field of brand building.

Addition of cultured products like yoghurt and cheese lend further strength - both in terms of utilization of resources and presence in the

the industry. Organized dissemination of information about the harm that they are doing to producers and consumers should see a steady decline in their importance.

The study of this SWOT analysis shows that the 'strengths' and 'opportunities' far outweigh 'weaknesses' and 'threats'. Strengths and opportunities are fundamental and weaknesses and threats are transitory. Any investment idea can do well only when you have three essential ingredients: entrepreneurship (the ability to take risks), an innovative approach (in product lines and marketing) and values (of quality/ethics).

The Indian dairy industry, following its delicensing, has been attracting a large number of entrepreneurs. Their success in dairying depends on factors such as an efficient yet economical procurement network, hygienic and cost-effective processing facilities and innovativeness in the market place. All that needs to be done is: to innovate, convert market place.

A lateral view opens up opportunities in milk proteins through casein, caseinates and other dietary proteins, further opening up export opportunities.

Yet another aspect can be the addition of infant foods, geriatric foods and nutritionals.

Export potential: Efforts to exploit export potential are already on. Amul is exporting to Bangladesh, Sri Lanka, Nigeria, and the Middle East. Following the new GATT treaty, opportunities will increase tremendously for the export of agri-products in general and dairy products in particular.

Questions

1. Explain the SWOT analysis of Indian diary.

products into commercially exploitable ideas. All the time keep reminding yourself: Benjamin Franklin discovered electricity, but it was the man who invented the meter that really made the money!

Source:http://www.indiadairy.com/ind_swot.html#Weaknesses

CHAPTER 6
TOWS MATRIX ANALYSIS

INTRODUCTION

Heinz Weihrich was developed a matrix called TOWS matrix by comparing strengths and weaknesses of the organization with that of market opportunities and threats. The Threats, Opportunities, Weaknesses and Strengths (TOWS) Matrix is an important matching tool that helps managers develop four types of strategies: SO Strategies, WO Strategies, ST Strategies, and WT Strategies. TOWS Matrix could be applied to the development of tactics necessary to implement the strategies, and to more specific actions supportive of tactics. It has been criticized that after conducting the SWOT analysis mangers frequently fail to come to terms with the strategic choices that the outcomes demand. TOWS inputs have recognized them and integrates them more fully into the strategic planning process. The matrix is listed below:

Figure- 6.1: The TOWS Matrix

Internal and External Factors	Organizational strengths	Organizational weaknesses
	Strategic options	
Environmental opportunities (and risks)	SO: Strengths can be used to capitalize or build upon existing or emerging opportunities	WO: the strategies developed need to overcome organizational weaknesses if existing or emerging opportunities are to be exploited
Environmental threats	ST: Strengths in the organization can be used to minimize existing or emerging	WT: the strategies pursued must minimize or overcome weaknesses and as far as

	threats	possible , cope with threats existing or emerging threats

PORTFOLIO ANALYSIS

Portfolio analysis is one of the magnificent analyses in order to current business portfolio; the company must conduct portfolio analysis to identify and evaluates the various businesses which make up the company. Top management views their product lines and business units relating to the portfolio analysis. It involves a series of investments in different products in different companies and expects a return from their investments. A business portfolio is a collection of businesses and products which make up the company. The best business portfolio is the one that appropriate to the company's strengths and weaknesses to opportunities in the business environment.

❖ The term portfolio analysis can be defined as "set of techniques that help to strategist in taking strategic decisions with regard to individual products or businesses in a firm's portfolio".

❖ It is primarily used for competitive analysis and corporate strategic planning in multi business firms in the market.

❖ It can be used in less diversified firms, these consist of the main business and other minor complementary interests.

Advantage of Portfolio Analysis

The significant advantages of portfolio analysis are outlined:

❖ It is a multi product approach.

❖ It involves investment in multi business firms.

❖ The investment could be channeled to different firms in the market.

❖ It helps investor minimize risk and maximize return from their investment in different companies.

❖ Its analysis and design the current business portfolio and decide which business should receive more, less or no investment in the business.

❖ There are three important concepts relating to portfolio analysis are outlined below:

  ▪ Strategic business units

  ▪ Product life cycle

  ▪ BCG group share matrix

Strategic Business Units

Some organizations encounter difficulty in controlling their divisional operations as the diversity, size, and the number of these units continues to increase. And corporate management may encounter difficulty in evaluating and controlling its numerous, often multi industry divisions. Under these conditions, it may become necessary to add another layer of management to improve strategy implementation, promoting synergy, and gain greater control over the diverse business interests. It can be achieved by grouping various divisions' in terms of common strategic elements. These groups commonly called strategic business units (SBUs)

❖ The strategic business unit   begins to identify key businesses also termed as a strategic business unit.

- ❖ SBU is a unit of the company. It has a separate mission and objectives.

- ❖ It can be planned independently of its mission, vision and objectives from other company businesses.

- ❖ The SBU can be a division of a company, it has a product line within a division or even a single product or brand.

- ❖ SBUs are common in organizations; these units are located in multiple countries with independent manufacturing and marketing setups.

Characteristics of SBUs

- ❖ Single business or collection of related businesses which can be planned for separately in different divisions across the global.

- ❖ It consists of competitors in the market.

- ❖ The division strategic manger is responsible person for strategic planning and profit of the company.

Advantages of SBUs Organizational Structure

- ❖ It improves coordination between divisions with similar strategic concerns and product / market environment.

- ❖ It tightens the strategic management and control of large, diverse business enterprises.

- ❖ It facilitates distinct and in depth business planning at the corporate and business levels.

- ❖ It Channels accountability to the distinct business unit.

Disadvantages of Strategic Business Unit Organizational Structure

- ❖ It places another layer of management between the divisions and corporate management.

- ❖ Its dysfunctional competition for corporate resource may increase.

- ❖ The role of the group vice president can be difficult to define.

- ❖ It is the difficulty in defining the degree of autonomy for the group vice presidents and division managers.

Experience Curve

- ❖ Experience curve is one of the important concepts.

- ❖ It is used for applying a portfolio approach.

- ❖ The concept is similar to a learning curve.

- ❖ It explains the efficiency increase and thereby gained workers through repetitive productive work.

- ❖ Experience curve is based on the commonly observed trend that costs decline as a firm accumulative experience in the form of a cumulative volume of production.

- ❖ It is implied that larger firms in an industry would tend to have lower unit costs as compared to those of smaller companies, thereby gaining competitive cost advantage in emerging markets.

- ❖ Experience curve results from a variety of factors like learning effects, economies of scale, product redesign, and technological improvements in production.

❖ It is applicable to various areas in strategic management. For instance, experience curve is considered a barrier for new firms contemplating entry in an industry and it used to build up market share and discourages competition.

Stages in Product / Market Evolution or Product Life Cycle

Product life cycle is the second factor to ascertainment of strengths and weakness of the organization. Stages in product life cycle are essential from the point of view of success of the organization. As a result, strategist can use changing patterns associated with different stages in product Lifecycle / market evolution as a framework for identifying and evaluating the organization's strengths and weakness. It is another important concept in strategic choice. This is a useful concept for guiding strategic choice.

There are four major stages of product life cycle / market evolution. PLC is an S – shaped curve which exhibits the relationship of sales with respect of time for a product that passes through the successive stages.
They are as below:

❖ Introduction stage is slow sales growth

❖ Growth stage is rapid market acceptance

❖ Maturity stage is a slowdown in growth rate and

❖ The decline / Saturation stage is sharp downward drift.

❖ And typical changes in functional capabilities often associated with business success at each stage of the development of the productive / market cycle.

Advantage of Product life Cycle

❖ It can be used to diagnose a portfolio of products or business in order to establish the stage at which each of them exists in business.

❖ Strengths are needed in the growth stage because of rapid growth brings competitor into the market. This stage involves with brand recognition, product or market differentiation and the financial resources to support both heavy marketing expenses and affect the price competition and effective cash flow can be key strengths at this stage.

❖ As the product/market moves through a "shake out" phases and into the maturity stage, this stage market growth continues but at a decreasing rate the number of market segments begins to expand, while technological change in product.

❖ Particular attention is to be paid on the businesses which are in the declining stage.

While the products markets move toward a saturation decline stage, this stage strengths and weakness center on the cost advantages, superior supplier or customer relationships and financial control. Product expansion is suitable for introduction and growth stages. Mature businesses stages are used as a source of cash investment in other businesses which needed resources. Harvesting, retrenchment strategies may be adopted for declining stage of businesses.

CHAPTER 7
BCG MATRIX

INTRODUCTION

Portfolio analysis is a significant exercise in corporate strategic planning. Investment and financial decisions should take into consideration the entire portfolio of the firm. It presents a framework for proper assessment of the capability of various operations of the company. The BCG model comes into play as a management analytical tool. BCG is the acronym for Boston Consulting Group-a general management consulting firm highly respected in business strategy consulting.

During the 1960s, a number of management consulting companies developed a series of conceptual techniques whose stated purpose was to help the top officers of diversified better management their portfolio of business. These techniques are known as portfolio planning techniques. Portfolio matrix first time developed by the Boston Consulting group which is named after them as BCG matrix. It can be used to classify product portfolio in four business types based on four graphic labels including Stars, Cash Cows, Question Marks and Dogs; it can be used to determine what priorities should be given in the product portfolio of a company; to classify an organization's product portfolio according to their cash usage and generation; and offers management available strategies to tackle various product lines.

Mission of BCG

BCG aims to help the world's best organizations make decisive improvements in their direction and performance by sparking breakthrough business ideas.

We see the essence of our work as a virtuous circle of insight, impact, and trust.

We continually strive to generate deep **insight** into what drives value creation and competitive advantage in our clients' businesses and the economy as a whole.

We work collaboratively with clients to convert insight into strategies that will have a substantial positive **impact** on performance.

Consistently delivering impact earns the **trust** that is the foundation of lasting relationships. These relationships serve as a platform for still deeper insight and more significant impact.

BCG seeks to stimulate continuous growth and success for our clients and, by doing so, to forge lifelong bonds with them.

The main objective of the Boston Consulting Group (BCG) technique is to help senior manager will identify the cash flow requirements of the different business in their portfolio. The BCG Growth – Share Matrix is based on two dimensional share matrixes. In the matrix:

❖ The vertical axis represents the relative market growth rate and provides a measure of market attractiveness.

❖ The horizontal axis represents a relative market share and serves as a measure of company strength in the market.

❖ Using the matrix, the organization can identify four different types of products or SBUs as follows:

Figure – 7.1:BCG Growth – Share Matrix

Source: 12manage.com

Stars

❖ Stars are leaders in high growth markets. Stars are products or SBUs that are growing rapidly.

❖ They tend to/should generate large amounts of cash (investment) but also use a lot of cash because of growth market conditions.

❖ They represent the best opportunities for expansion.

Cash Cows

- ❖ These products are said to have high profitability.

- ❖ These require low investment.

- ❖ They are market leaders in a low-growth market.

- ❖ They are established, successful, and need less investment to maintain their market share.

Question Marks

- ❖ Question Marks have not achieved a dominant market position.

- ❖ And hence do not generate much cash.

- ❖ They tend to use a lot of cash because of growth market conditions.

Dogs

- ❖ Dogs often have little future.

- ❖ And are big cash drainers on the company.

- ❖ They generate very little cash by virtue of their low market share in a highly low growth market.

AVAILABLE STRATEGIES TO PURSUE

There are four strategies available to pursue:

Build

- ❖ The product or SBU's market share needs to be increased to strengthen its position.

- ❖ Short-term earnings and profits are deliberately forfeited because it is hoped that the long-term gains will be higher than this.

❖ This strategy is suited to Question Marks if they are to become stars.

Hold

❖ The objective is to maintain the current share position and this strategy is often used for Cash Cows so that they continue to generate large amounts of cash.

Harvest

❖ Here management tries to increase short-term cash flows as far as possible (e.g. price increase, cutting costs) even at the expense of the products or SBU's longer-term future.

❖ It is a strategy suited to weak Cash Cows or Cash Cows that are in a market with a limited future.

❖ Harvesting is also used for Question Marks where there is no possibility of turning them into Stars, and for Dogs.

Divest

❖ The objective of this strategy is to rid the organization of the products or SBUs that are a drain on profits and to utilize these resources elsewhere in the business where they will be of greater benefit.

❖ This strategy is typically used for Question Marks that will not become Stars and for Dogs.

Limitations of the BCG Matrix

❖ It is Cleary defining a market is a very difficult task as a result, accurately measuring share and growth rate can be a problem. This creates the potential manipulation or distortion.

❖ Dividing the matrix into four cells is based on a high /low classification scheme.

❖ It does not recognize the markets with average growth rates or the business with an average market share.

❖ The relationship between market share and profitability underlying BCG matrix.

❖ The BCG matrix is not particularly helpful in comparing relative investment opportunities across different business units in the corporate portfolio.

❖ Strategic evaluation of a set of business requires examination of more than relative market shares and market growth.

ANSOFF'S PRODUCT - MARKET GROWTH MATRIX

The Ansoff's product growth matrix is a useful tool which helps businesses decide their product and market growth strategy. This matrix, developed by H. Igor Ansoff, is a handy tool for thinking about how its growth depends upon it markets in new or existing products in a both new and existing markets. Companies always looking for a better future, companies are identifying the growth opportunities for the future of their product and market. It should be noted that this is an environment led process which sees the company's market situation as a leading feature. It may not be suitable in a situation of a contracting market.

The matrix shows the major choices that available to companies, faces in its mission for growth and opportunities in the future. The company can be targeted to new or existing markets with new or existing products.

The results- in the boxes, these boxes are suggested routes for the company's growth strategy.

Figure – 7.2: Ansoff's Matrix

	Present Product	New Product
Present Market	Market Penetration	Product Development
New Market	Market Development	Diversification

Present   New

Product

Market Penetration
* A market penetration strategy refers to growth strategy when the company will aim to sell its existing products within its existing markets that it already serves but in greater numbers.
* This will entail a greater effort in sales and marketing to achieve higher product sales, in this way achieve the greater market share.
* This can be achieved through improving the products quality and/ or by productivity gains leading to cost reductions.
* It might require greater spending on advertising or personal selling.

❖ Over competition in a mature market that requires an aggressive promotional campaign which supported by a pricing strategy designed to make the market unattractive for competitors in market.

❖ It is also done by increasing the customer base for their products and services.

Product Development

❖ A product development strategy entails developing new products for sale in existing markets.

❖ It aims to introduce new products into existing markets.

❖ This strategy for company growth by offering modified or new products to current markets.

❖ It requires the new development of new competencies and requires the business to develop modified products that can be appealed to existing markets.

Market Development

❖ Market development refers to growth strategy which occurs when a company attempts to sell its existing products into new markets.

❖ It is a strategy for company its growth by identifying and developing new markets for current company products and services.

❖ This strategy achieved through the new geographic market, new product dimensions or packaging, new distribution channels or different pricing policies to attract different customers or create new market segments.

Diversification

❖ Diversification refers to growth strategy that to occur when a company decides to sell newly developed products within a new market.

❖ It is strategy by starting up or acquiring businesses outside the company's current products and markets.

❖ It involves risk due to introducing new products into new market.

❖ Generally, the business is moving into markets in which it has little or some time no experience.

❖ There is a wide range of possibilities for achieving this strategy but they fall into two main groups are related and unrelated diversification.

❖ **Related diversification** involves developing new products to sell in new markets but within the same industry or broad area as before.

❖ **Unrelated diversification** occurs when a company decides to enter a new business area as well as develop new products and finding new customers.

ADL MATRIX

It is a combination of the two aforementioned dimensions that helps us to use ADL for marketing decision-making. Now let's consider options in more detail. Competitive position has five main categories;

Competitiv e position	Stage in Industry maturity			
	Embryonic	Growth	Mature	Ageing
Dominant	Fast grow Build barriers act offensively	Fast grow attend cost leadership renew defend position act offensively	Defend a position attend cost leadership renew fast grow act offensively	Defend a position Renew Focus consider withdrawal
Strong	Differentiat e fast grow	Differentiat e lower cost attack small firms	Lower cost focus differentiat e grow	Find niche hold niche harvest

			with industry	
Favourable	Differentiate focus grow	Focus differentiate defend	Focus differentiate harvest find niche hold niche turnaround grow with industry hit smaller firms	Harvest turnaround
Teanable	Growth with industry focus	Hold niche turnaround focus grow with industry withdraw	Turnaround hold niche retrench	Divest retrench
Weak	Find niche catch up grow with industry	Turnaround retrench niche or withdraw	Withdraw divest	withdraw

Dominant

❖ This is particularly extraordinary position.

❖ Often this is associated with some form of monopoly position or customer lock-in e.g. Microsoft Windows being the dominant global operating system

Strong

❖ Here companies have a lot of freedom since position in an industry is comparatively powerful e.g. Apple's iPod products

Favourable

- ❖ Companies with a favourable position tend to have competitive strengths in segments of a fragmented market place.
- ❖ No single global player controls all segments.
- ❖ Here product strengths and geographical advantages come into play.

Tenable

- ❖ companies may face erosion by stronger competitors that have a favourable, strong or competitive position.
- ❖ It is difficult for them to compete since they do not have a sustainable competitive advantage.

Weak

- ❖ The performance of firms in this category is generally unsatisfactory although the opportunity for improvement does exist in the market.
- ❖ Of course there are opportunities to change and improve, and therefore to take an organization to a more favourable, strong or even dominant position.

The General Electric model

The general Electric Model developed by GE with assistance of the Mckinsey consulting and Company. It is similar to the BCG growth share matrix. So that, there are differences are outlined below:

- ❖ Market attractiveness replaces market growth, it one of the dimensions of industry attractiveness It includes a broader range of factors rather than just the market rate.
- ❖ Competitive strengths replaces market share, it is one of the dimensions by which the competitive position of each strategic business unit is assessed

Figure- 7.3: Criteria for rating business Position and market Attractiveness

Evaluating the ability to compete : Business Position	Evaluating the Market Attractiveness
Size Growth Share by segment Customer loyalty Margins Distribution Technology skills Patents Markcting Flexibility Organization	Size Growth Customer satisfaction levels Competition : quality , types Effectiveness, commitment Price levels Profitability Technology Government regulations Sensitivity to economic trends

In this figure, we shall consider the rate of market attractiveness and business position assigned different ways in the organization. Therefore, some criteria are more important than others. The each SBU is rated with respect to all criteria in this figure, finally, overall rating for both factors are calculated for SBU in the organization. Based on these ratings factors, each SBU is labeled as high, medium or low with respect to a market attractiveness and business position.

Every business organization has to make decisions regards about how to use its limited resources. It most effectively applicable to where these planning models can help to determine in which SBU should be stimulated for growth, which one maintained in their present market position and which one eliminated.

ABOUT THE AUTHOR

Dr.B. Hiriyappa, is a Ph.D, He is a prolific author of 16 books: Strategic Management, Strategic Management for Chartered Accountant, Investment Management, Organizational Behavior, business environment, Business Policy and Strategic Management, Strategic Management and Business Policy : For Managers and Consultants.25 E books are Strategic Analysis, Strategic Planning, Formulation of Functional Strategy, Business Environment, Business Policy and Strategic management etc.

www.ingramcontent.com/pod-product-compliance
Lightning Source LLC
Chambersburg PA
CBHW081223170526
45165CB00009B/2933